Moscata Visits a Monastery

Chelsea Youell

ST VLADIMIR'S SEMINARY PRESS • YONKERS • NEW YORK • 2021

Hello! My name is Moscata. Join me as I venture through this women's monastery. I am excited to show you around!

A monastery is a community of nuns or monks who have devoted their lives entirely to God. Here, nuns, monks, and visitors can learn more about God and his will for our lives.

Look! Two Orthodox nuns, Mother and Abbess Mother live here. They take very good care of the monastery.

Nuns are female monastics.

Monks are male monastics.

A monastic is someone who has chosen to direct their full life to Christ by "laying aside all earthly cares" and living a life of prayer and work.

Abbess (female) or abbot (male) is a title given to the superior of a monastic community.

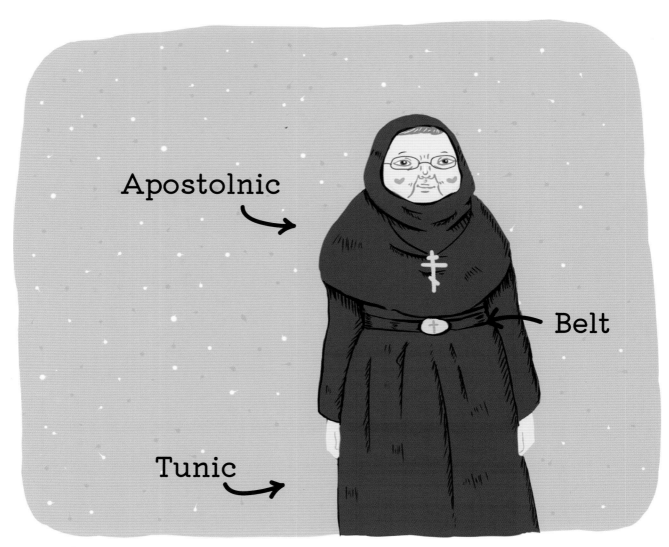

Apostolnic

Belt

Tunic

You might be wondering about the nuns' clothing.

This is the monastic habit, also known as their burial shroud. Black symbolizes their own death to this world. They remember death daily to help spiritually prepare themselves for the future. Here are the different parts of the habit.

A tunic is a loose-fitting dress.

A belt is worn over the tunic. It depicts the crucifixion and symbolizes being "girded with strength" from God.

An apostolnic is a head covering.

Klobuk

Veil

Outer riassa

Mantia

This is the liturgical garb, worn during church services. Here is what each piece is called.

The klobuk is a stiff hat worn on top of the head, also known as the helmet of salvation.

Over the hat, a veil is worn. Veils symbolize purity, resistance towards temptation, and a guard against vanity.

The outer riassa is a wide-sleeved outer robe.

A mantia is a long cape with 33 pleats on each side. The pleats represent the number of years Christ walked the Earth.

Apart from worship, monastics also practice the Orthodox tradition of fasting. I love fasting days, because they give me more celery in my dish!

Fasting is the removal or limitation of food. Examples of food not eaten when fasting are meats, dairy, and olive oil. This builds self control and discipline. Fasting also allows more time for prayer.

Prayer is uniting yourself to Jesus Christ in your body, mind, and heart. It is a time to praise God, give thanks, seek help, and ask for forgiveness. It is important to pray every day.

"Lord Jesus Christ, Son of God, have mercy on me, a sinner."

Monastics pray constantly. The most common prayer said is the Jesus Prayer. This nun is using a prayer rope while she prays.

Monastics pray for the salvation of the whole world. They also pray for themselves and those who ask for prayer.

The Jesus prayer is one of the most important Orthodox prayers. A common version of the prayer is "Lord Jesus Christ, Son of God, have mercy on me, a sinner."

A prayer rope consists of a varying number of knots. These knots are used to count how many times the Jesus Prayer has been said.

Mother and Abbess Mother chose to follow the path of monasticism.

There is a forest at the monastery. It is full of different paths to follow, and each leads to a new interesting place.

Let us see where they go. Follow me!

One path leads to the candle shop. This building is named after Saint Joseph the Betrothed.

Saint Joseph the Betrothed was the guardian of the Virgin Mary who gave birth to Christ the Son of God. He trusted God and protected Mary and her Son, acting like a husband and father.

In this building, the nuns make beeswax candles of various sizes. This takes both time and patience. It smells heavenly in here!

Beeswax comes from bee hives and gives off a light, sweet smell. It can be molded into different shapes. The candles that the nuns make are used by Orthodox Christians at home and in the church.

Orthodox Christians use candles at home for prayer. In church, candles are lit in prayer during services, such as Divine Liturgy. The leftover wax can be returned to the monastery to help make more candles.

Divine Liturgy means the common act or work of the people. It is where the community of the Church comes together and hears the Word of God and receives Holy Communion. Divine Liturgy is always held on Sunday, the Lord's day, and on Christian feast days.

These candles are also sold in the monastery store. The store is located in the Barne Shoppe building. This building is dedicated to Saint Brigid of Kildare.

Saint Brigid of Kildare was a devoted nun in Ireland who worked many miracles, such as helping a blind man see. During her life, she helped serve God while giving what she could to the poor, building a monastery, and taking care of the monastics who lived there.

Miracles are amazing events that exceed the Law of Nature, defeat it, and surprise reason. Miracles are the acts of God.

The monastery store sells other items such as books, icons, prayer ropes, jewelry, and more. The store helps the nuns earn money so the monastery can continue to grow.

Icons are holy images that represent holy people, like Jesus Christ, the Virgin Mary, or the saints. They can also show angels or events from the Bible. Icons have been used by Christians in churches and for prayer for almost two thousand years. Some icons have been known to work miracles, even to this very day.

The Barne Shoppe building also includes a greenhouse room where many beautiful plants are tended. The nuns take time and care to nurture each plant. It is very calm here. It's the perfect place to curl up next to the window and take a nap.

Near the monastery home, there is an orchard where various trees and bushes grow and produce fruit. Ducks can be seen roaming about. They help keep bugs away from the fruit and lay eggs for the nuns. I want to chase and play with the ducks, but they prefer to be left alone in peace while they work.

Here is our monastery garden where the nuns grow and harvest vegetables. Many monastics work hard and perform manual tasks such as this. Monastics pray before, during, and after every work.

Home-grown food always tastes the best. I really enjoy celery whenever it's handpicked!

Nearby is another garden, the flower garden. The lovely plants and benches here make this a quiet place to pray, and reflect on the beauty of God's creation. This is a perfect place to bathe in the sun during the warmer weather. Now, let me show you some new friends!

The monastery cats are here! Their names are Mancini and Makiko.

Look at these cheery birds! There are bird feeders that hang near trees, and bird baths below that attract nearby animals.

No need to worry about Mancini and Makiko. They get along with the wildlife and are too well fed for unnecessary hunting.

The monastery holds much life and offers a place for the reposed. A graveyard is kept and maintained on the monastery grounds. People come here to bless and pray for those who have passed away.

Reposed (or those who have "fallen asleep") refers to those who have died, but still live in Christ.

Sometimes when people come to visit, they choose to stay at the hermitage. This hermitage is dedicated to Theotokos the Eldress.

A hermitage is a place of solitude and meditation away from the noisiness of the outside world.

Theotokos the Eldress is an icon of the Theotokos that shows her as an abbess. The original icon has been known to work many miracles.

Theotokos is a Greek name for the Mother of God, or the Virgin Mary; meaning "God-Bearer," the one who gave birth to God.

The hermitage is a simple home free from distractions. This creates the perfect environment for prayer and silent reflection.

I can come here to get away from the cats, Makiko and Mancini!

While walking through the woods, visitors can stop and pray before an icon of Christ. This is a wonderful outside icon that can be venerated.

Veneration is the act of showing respect to what is holy. Icon veneration can include kissing or bowing. Orthodox Christians do not worship icons. Icons are not the saints, the Virgin Mary, or Christ himself. Icons portray these holy figures, which is why they are shown much respect and love.

Inside the monastery home, there is a small chapel. There are two chapels on the monastery grounds. You can find the first one here.

Icons are displayed on the wall and a crucifix stands in the center. The nuns pray and worship here every day.

A chapel is where the services of the church are held, such as Divine Liturgy, vespers, and matins.

The crucifix is a display of Christ on the Cross. This shows the suffering and sacrifice he endured for us all.

At times incense is used with icons. I enjoy seeing the smoke fill the room. Censers hang near icons as they are venerated. Here, a nun is prostrating before an icon.

Incense is created by adding small scented pieces of resin to a censer, and then deacons or priests swing the censer in church services. Both icons and people at the services are censed with this smoke. It symbolizes prayer as the smoke rises up to God.

Prostration is an act of falling down before God in repentance. Orthodox Christians pray standing, kneeling, and in prostration. This act of prayer has been kept by Orthodox Christians throughout the ages.

The monastery is growing quickly! A new building is being built to house more people and hold services. Donations and spiritual support have helped make this possible.

The nuns also appreciate the kindness given by volunteers. Taking care of a monastery can be a lot of work, and is easier with the help of others!

Donating is the selfless act of giving money, goods, time, or talent (to a cause).

Volunteering is willing to do a task without being asked or paid.

This new building will give more room for additional nuns, and an open place for worship. The bigger chapel is located in this building.

Here, people can come for liturgies and services with the nuns.

Visiting with the nuns, I understand the beauty and spiritual fulfillment that comes with living a monastic lifestyle. Monastics give up the things of this world so that nothing stands between them and God.

They live a life of obedience, chastity, poverty, and stability. They have few material possessions to distract or worry them. For example, I do not need toys and treats. God provides us with all that we need!

Life is sacred, and true life is found in Christ. Living a monastic life may seem difficult, but it is difficult for a reason.

We bear our cross as Christ did. We must work out our salvation. By surrendering our life to Christ, we find happiness.

In love and prayer we offer hospitality and spiritual refreshment to those whom God leads to us. I hope you are able to come by a monastery to visit soon!

Mancini

Makiko

Moscata here! Thank you so much for reading my book! Your support goes a long way!

From left to right: Mother Lubov of blessed memory, the Abbess Mother Thecla, and Mother Helena with women from one of the Clergy Wives Retreats.

This book is dedicated to Saints Mary and Martha Orthodox Monastery in Wagener, SC. To the wonderful nuns that reside there, thank you for being the inspiration of this book and for all of the love that you have shown me. May the Lord continue to send forth his blessings upon this monastery.

– C.Y.

Chelsea Youell is the author and illustrator of this book!

Born and raised in South Carolina, she graduated from USCA with a degree in Fine Arts. When she discovered the beauty of Orthodoxy, she decided to express this through art. She plans to create Orthodox books for children in order to spread interest in the Orthodox faith.

ST VLADIMIR'S SEMINARY PRESS

575 Scarsdale Road, Yonkers, New York 10707

www.svspress.com • 1-800-204-2665

Text and illustrations copyright © 2021 Chelsea Youell

ISBN 978-0-88141-696-1

LIBRARY OF CONGRESS CONTROL NUMBER: 2021942047

Printed in China

To learn more about the Saints Mary and Martha Orthodox Monastery, Wagener, SC, visit www.saintsmaryandmarthaorthodoxmonastery.org.